Van Gogh

Van Gogh

Text and Notes by
GERALD E. FINLEY
Acting Head, Department of Art History
Queen's University, Canada

TUDOR PUBLISHING COMPANY
New York

All rights reserved

TUDOR PUBLISHING COMPANY,

New York, 1966

Library of Congress Catalog Card Number : 66-10490

Printed in Japan

VAN GOGH, PAINTER OF THE SUN

The brilliance and violence of Vincent van Gogh's canvases remain mute reminders of a short and tragic life. Van Gogh was a misfit in a world that could not appreciate his genius until after his death. From early youth he had lived passionately, impulsively, reaching out for vague, unattainable goals, trusting his innermost thoughts to strangers; and while he sometimes received sympathy, he more often suffered indifference and rejection from those around him. He stands today as the archetype of the neglected genius.

On March 30, 1853, Van Gogh was born at Groot-Zundert in the district of North-Brabant in Holland, near the Belgian border, a bleak region in which the plight of the peasant was to be one of his earliest and strongest impressions. In many ways his childhood was normal and uneventful. He was the eldest of six children born into a warm and affectionate household. His father, a Protestant minister, was a gentle and considerate man who perhaps hoped that his son would one day follow one of the professions that had distinguished the family for generations. His forebears had been clergymen and successful men of business.

Yet the young Vincent gave indications that he would not be well suited to either profession. An extremely sensitive boy, he was a victim of frequent moods of depression. Fortunately, his family provided a good measure of the stability, affection and understanding that he so desperately needed. Vincent was particularly fond of his brother Theo, four years younger, who was to be his only source of spiritual as well as financial succor in the later years.

In 1869, at the age of sixteen, Vincent was recommended by an uncle for a clerical post in an art gallery in The Hague, one of many operated throughout western Europe by the Paris firm of Goupil and Company. At first he worked with great efficiency, but his long silences and irritability prevented the growth of any close relationships with his associates. As a result, he sought reassurance and companionship in a correspondence with Theo—a correspondence that was to continue unabated until his death. In his letters to his brother he confided his deepest thoughts, and his trust and love for Theo were reciprocated and, more important, demonstrated by the care with which Theo responded to these letters.

In 1873 Vincent was transferred to the branch of the Goupil firm in London, where he experienced his first tragic love affair. He fell in love with his landlady's daughter. When he finally summoned up courage to ask her to marry him, he was immediately rebuffed and informed that she was already engaged. This must have been shortly before July 1874, for it was then that he returned to Holland for the holidays. His parents found him thin and depressed; his first encounter with a woman had left him utterly defeated.

It was during 1874 and 1875 that Van Gogh developed a deep interest in religion. In the later months of 1874 he had returned to work at the Goupil office in Paris, where he spent his evenings reading the Bible with a young Englishman. In the winter of that year he was again sent to London. Once more he went to the landlady's daughter, pleading with her to marry him; a second time she rejected him. Distraught, he sought escape in a frenzy of reading and religious meditation. When he returned to

Goupil and Company

Letters to Theo

Rejection and religious fervor

Paris in the spring of 1875 to resume his duties at Goupil's, his interest in religion was fervid. He found it difficult to concentrate on his work and was continually arguing with his colleagues. The office atmosphere become so unbearable that he was asked to leave.

It was in April, 1876, that he was given his discharge from Goupil's. He left almost immediately to take up a teaching post at Ramsgate on the south coast of England, where he was given his keep but earned no salary. He had been hired to instruct in French and German but did not prove very capable as teacher. A short time later, when the school was moved to Isleworth in the suburbs of London, Van Gogh, feeling the need of a salary, left for another position in a school run by a clergyman. Here he often performed the duties of a sort of curate and came to the realization that he could probably serve society better as a preacher or missionary than as a pedagogue. At Christmas, heartened by this new thought, he returned to the home of his parents, now at Etten.

Attempts at teaching

For a few months in early 1877, he worked as a clerk in a Dordrecht bookshop. Here in relative quiet he found emotional respite; and spent hours in the evenings reading theology and philosophy in the hope of preparing himself for a career in the ministry. Encouraged by his father, he decided to sit for the divinity entrance examinations to be held in Amsterdam.

In Amsterdam, he studied continuously for fourteen months, poring over the difficult philosophy of Calvin as well as wrestling with Greek and Latin which he could not seem to master. In July of 1878 he gave up. His abilities, he felt, lay not in scholarship but in the practical application of the Gospel. Later in the year, however, he decided to try again. This time he was admitted to a lay evangelical school in Brussels, where the curriculum was designed

The ministry

to give the rudiments of the Gospel and preaching to laymen, whose task it would then be to bring the word of Christ to the forgotten miners, factory workers and peasants working on the land. Van Gogh was not considered very good missionary material, but he was permitted to seek out his own congregation. He chose the poor district of the Borinage, South of Mons, near the French border. Here, he preached to local miners.

The Borinage

Deliberately he identified himself with his congregation. To be one of them, to endure the same indignations and privations, he occupied a hut, slept on bare planks and refused to wash. Filled with compassion for these neglected people, he rushed frantically about the villages of the area, tending the sick and reading the Bible when the opportunity presented itself. But his wild-looking, unwashed figure only alarmed and finally aroused the suspicions of these simple folk. After completing a probationary period at Wasmes he was dismissed by the organization in Brussels. He was unprepared for and utterly shattered by the blow.

While he was encouraged to remain in the Borinage at his own expense, it is clear from his letters that he began to have serious doubts about his profession. Religious reflections and quotations which had previously filled his letters now became noticeably absent. Dejected, he withdrew from society and began to sketch the countryside and its inhabitants. His ability to draw had developed at quite an early age and he had always shown an interest in art.

Early sketches

For nearly a year he traveled and sketched, but in the summer of 1880 his wanderings ceased, and his mind cleared—he would be an artist. At Cuesmes he busied himself drawing workers and peasants and undertook a number of copies of Millet's *Sower*.

At the end of August, 1881, Vincent was at the home of his family at Etten. Here he fell in love again, this time with his cousin Kee, a young widow who did not return his affection. Eventually he left home again, filled with a sense of defeat and frustration.

From Etten he made his way to The Hague where he received encouragement from his artist cousin, Anton Mauve, who suggested that he study art. Theo, who was contributing money to his support, also gave him his full sympathy and encouragement for the new profession.

It was in The Hague in 1882 that Van Gogh formed another strong attachment with a woman; this time a prostitute. The artist found her ill and pregnant in the street and with a compassion he had already shown for the downtrodden, took her home, offering her a new life both as model and mistress. Her name was Christien but he was to call her Sien. The thought of having a home and family clearly delighted him, but it was soon apparent that his happiness could not last. Sien proved spiteful and managed to squander his meagre allowance from Theo. Although he held to her tenaciously, he was finally persuaded by Theo to break the liaison. During his rather unsettled life with Sien, he drew *Sorrow*, a poignant study of his mistress, head in hands, which reflects utter despair.

Van Gogh left The Hague and the memories of Sien in December of 1883, forlorn and stunned. He returned to his parents' home, now in the eastern part of North-Brabant at Nuenen. For two years he worked with vigor and determination, sympathetically painting the peasants in the sullen harmonies of the earth and country from which they eked a meagre living. From the innumerable oil studies and pencil sketches made at this time, he shaped the brooding canvas, the *Potato Eaters* (6).

However, while the paintings of this period are dark and heavy, Van Gogh was clearly showing an interest in color theory. He was attracted to ideas of complementary

9

colors espoused by Eugene Delacroix. In a letter to Theo he noted that "one has to put very little yellow into a color to make it seem very yellow if one puts that color in or next to a violet or a lilac tone." Later he suggested that Theo himself should study Delacroix's theory and regrets that the laws of color were not taught during his youth. During the Nuenen period Vincent first began to realize, at least in theory, the expressive potential of color: "Color expresses something in itself, one cannot do without this, one must use it."

Not all went favorably for Van Gogh during this period. Another unfortunate love affair occurred in which the girl was driven to attempted suicide by her disapproving family. A further blow was the sudden death of his father.

It was in Antwerp in the latter part of 1885 and early 1886 that Vincent experienced the rich color effects of the paintings of Rubens and Japanese woodblock prints. These influences were eventually to lead him to reject the deep and gloomy hues of his Nuenen period. At Antwerp he enrolled in the Academy but soon felt dissatisfied with the teaching and left for Paris to stay with Theo, who was employed in the Goupil head office.

By attending the Cormon studio in Paris, Vincent came to know Toulouse-Lautrec and Emile Bernard. Through Theo and the paint dealer Père Tanguy, he also came in contact with the Impressionists; he was introduced to Cézanne and Gauguin, and learned of Neo-Impressionist color theory being practiced by Seurat, Signac and Pissarro. The Impressionists and Neo-Impressionists were absorbed by the study of light and attempted to capture its effects in their paintings by means of small strokes or dots of intense color. Van Gogh's palette was greatly influenced by their color and he adopted certain qualities of their style of painting. He painted canvases such as *A Corner of Montmartre* (9) in which rich colors are applied as long slender threads which sketch in landscape forms. In *The Restaurant* (15), the painting is constructed of tiny dots of complementary hues as in the Neo-Impressionist technique.

In 1888 an ill Van Gogh left Paris, unable to sell his paintings, and traveled to Arles in the south of France. In this environment his palette took on a new splendor. It was here that he found true emotional release through brilliant color. And it was here that he felt he could depict the color of the South that burned on Delacroix's canvases. He wished to display "the rich color and rich sun of the glorious South in a true colorist way parallel with Delacroix's conception of the South viz. that the South be represented now by contraste simultané of colors and their derivations and harmonies and not by forms and lines themselves as the ancient artists did formerly...."

Van Gogh found in Arles a brilliance of light such as Delacroix found in Africa, "beautiful contrasts of red and green, of blue and orange, of sulphur and lilac." He was particularly attracted by yellow, and felt it the dominant color of the South. "Just now we are having a glorious strong heat, with no wind, just what I want. There is a sun, a light that for want of a better word I can only call yellow, pale sulphur yellow, pale golden citron. How lovely yellow is!" But while he was concerned with sunlight he was not always interested, as were the Impressionists, in the way sunlight affected the appearance of things. He was more concerned with the sun itself, as a symbol—a personal symbol. As a consequence he executed in this period numerous works, usually strongly yellow in hue, in which the sun played a prominent part; if not a sun then its equivalent, a sunflower, or burning stars in a night sky, or the yellow effulgence of a lantern.

It was a period of intense activity for Van Gogh. He felt a new freedom which he confided to Theo in his letters. Some of the works of this period most brilliant in hue are *The Night Café* (37) and *The Sower* (39). Here paint is now applied in large patches of intense color. As he observed in discussing one of his bedroom scenes, "No stippling, no hatching, nothing, only flat colors in harmony."

Gauguin

Eager to establish an artists' colony in Arles, he begged Paul Gauguin to come and live with him. Both artists, he felt, could benefit from each other's knowledge and support. While awaiting Gauguin's arrival, he busied himself making everything comfortable in the little yellow house he had rented. The older artist arrived in October of 1888, but although the two men tried to live together in harmony, it was soon clear that their personalities were quite incompatible.

After frequent quarrels, including a violent altercation at the local café on Christmas Eve, Gauguin decided to leave. Van Gogh broke under the strain of the decision. Gauguin had gone strolling just before his departure on the evening after the quarrel at the café; suddenly he heard someone behind him, and, turning, saw Van Gogh about to attack him with a razor. With a few words and a contemptuous stare, he forced Van Gogh to retreat.

Break-down and confine-ment

Struck with remorse, Van Gogh fled to his room where he took a fit, sliced off the lobe of his own ear and delivered it to a brothel he frequented.

Van Gogh was taken to a hospital in a delirious condition. Theo arrived from Paris, having received a telegram from Gauguin who by this time had left Arles, not wishing to have more to do with this strange Dutchman. After a few weeks Van Gogh recovered and by early January of 1889 was well enough to leave. It was at this time that he executed his *Self-Portrait with Bandaged Ear* (53). In

January and February he was busily painting in spite of minor attacks. He realized that he was not completely well and confided to Theo, "When I came out of the hospital with kind old Roulin, who had come to get me, I thought that there had been nothing wrong with me, but *afterward* I felt that I had been ill. Well, well, there are moments when I am twisted by enthusiasm or madness or prophecy, like a Greek oracle on the tripod." His life was further upset at the end of February. The townspeople, fearing for their safety with a "madman" in their midst, petitioned the mayor to have him recommitted. In detention his spirits fell, but he was cheered somewhat when the painter Signac came to visit him and with sincerity praised his work.

Saint Rémy

Van Gogh finally realized the seriousness of his illness and voluntarily requested that he be transferred to the asylum for the insane at Saint-Rémy. Here he could expect better treatment for his affliction and would at the same time be of less trouble and expense to Theo, who was about to be married. He arrived at Saint-Rémy in May of 1889.

The doctor of the hospital at Arles, Dr. Rey, had been one of the first to recognize Van Gogh's genius. When the artist entered the Saint-Rémy asylum, Dr. Rey recommended to Dr. Peyron, its chief physician, that Van Gogh be allowed to paint as often as possible and that he receive special privileges. His love for the sun and starry nights unabated, the artist painted landscapes outside the asylum walls, fields, landscapes with cypress trees, mountains and olive orchards. When forced to remain indoors either because of poor health or bad weather, he copied paintings of the masters, especially Delacroix, Daumier, Rembrandt and Millet. On many occasions he was in poor spirits. He wrote to his brother, "Only I have no news to tell you, for the days are all the same, I have no ideas, except to think that a field of wheat or a cypress is well worth the trouble

Increasing depression

13

of looking at close up and so on." It was at Saint-Rémy that he became especially attracted to cypress trees. "The cypress are always occupying my thoughts, I should like to make something of them like the canvases of sunflowers, because it astonishes me that they have not yet been done as I see them." It was also at Saint-Rémy that his style changed. While the colors of his canvases executed here were less brilliant than those painted in Arles, a new expressive force had been introduced. Landscape forms became contorted, the topography and cloud forms began to writhe and trees took on a rhythmic flame-like appearance as his painting became an emotional substitute for normal relations. Most typical of the works of this period are *Starry Night* (59) and *View with Olive Trees* (65).

Auvers-sur-Oise and death

In May of 1890, Vincent, at Theo's urging, moved to Auvers-sur-Oise, near Paris. Here he became a patient of Dr. Gachet, himself an amateur painter and friend of such artists as Pissarro and Cézanne. Dr. Gachet encouraged Vincent to paint and talk about art. The artist, in better spirits, began to work enthusiastically on landscapes and executed several portraits of Dr. Gachet and his daughter. The rippling undulations of the paintings of the Saint Rémy period are intensified, as for example in the powerful and foreboding *Wheatfield with Crows* (88). In July of this year a new attack may have been threatening, for Vincent wrote Theo that "the prospect grows darker, I see no happy future at all." He obtained a revolver on some pretext and on Sunday, the 27th of July, stood in a field and shot a bullet into his chest. He survived two days. Less than six months later Theo joined him in death.

BRIEF BIBLIOGRAPHY

Vincent van Gogh

The Complete Letters of Vincent van Gogh. Thames and Hudson, London, 1958.

La Faille, J.-B. de: *Vincent van Gogh.* Paris, 1939.

Gans, L.: *Vincent van Gogh: 1853–1890.* Exhibition Haus de Kunst, Munich, 1956.

Nordenfalk, C.: *Vincent van Gogh.* London, 1947.

Shapiro, M.: *Vincent van Gogh.* New York, 1950.

NOTES ON THE COLOR PLATES

1, 2. *The Weaver* and *The Loom*. 1884. Oil. *The Weaver* is in a private collection, Berlin; *The Loom* is in the Rijksmuseum Kröller-Müller, Otterlo. In the drab town of Nuenen, with its 2500 inhabitants, the passionate young artist felt at home with these people of the earth, though they hardly reciprocated his warmth of feeling. Van Gogh was fascinated by the weavers and their looms. In January of 1884 he wrote Theo about the pictorial effects that could be achieved with them. He was particularly interested in the unusual lighting created under gas lamps which could produce "Rembrandt-like effects." *The Weaver* is a study made by lamplight. Van Gogh spoke also of silhouetting the loom and weaver against the light walls of the cottage interiors. Such an effect is captured in *The Loom*.

3. *Snowy Day*. 1884. Oil. Private Collection, Laren. This is based on a similar theme by Millet, a source of inspiration to Van Gogh throughout his painting career. Browns, blacks and coarse textures seem to obsess the artist and against the white snow emphasize the starkness of the peasant's daily life.

4. *Still-Life with Hat and Pipe*. 1884. Oil. Rijksmuseum Kröller-Müller, Otterlo. New colors appear on Van Gogh's palette, although he still subdues brightness by employing brown and black backgrounds. He wrote Theo that these still-life paintings were primarily color studies. Such subjects were to occupy him throughout his career.

5. *Peasant Woman*. 1885. Private Collection, Zurich. The Brabant of Holland is the country's poorest section. From it Van Gogh had come, and here the artist began to paint its inhabitants with great compassion. The peasant heads of this period capture the pathos and depth

of feeling that can be found in the portraits of Rembrandt, Van Gogh's spiritual ancestor. Van Gogh felt that his paintings of peasants should stimulate the thought of those who "think seriously about art and life."

6. *The Potato Eaters*. 1885. Oil. Vincent van Gogh Foundation, Laren. The artist's famous remark, "I wanted to show the peasants eating something which they had dug from the ground with their bare hands," typifies the deep understanding Van Gogh had for the weary monotony and despair of the peasants' lives. Their hands are gnarled and seemingly incapable of fine gesture, yet their dignity is captured in the gloom of the poorly-lit hovel.

7. *The Open Bible*. 1885. Oil. Vincent van Gogh Foundation, Laren. The relief which Van Gogh sought all his life from religion it seemed was at an end, never to be granted him. His well-intentioned attempt to preach the Gospel came to nothing and he was to feel himself rejected by God and men the rest of his days. The rich paint texture, the slashing brushstrokes, in many ways prefigure his later style.

8. *Montmartre*. 1886. Oil. Art Institute, Chicago. When Van Gogh reached Antwerp he encountered Japanese prints for the first time. When he came to Paris, the Japanese print and Impressionism and Neo-Impressionism were to help form his new style. This work with its variety of free brushwork indicates both the skeletal structure of Japanese prints and the free fluid strokes and silvery tones of the Impressionists.

9. *A Corner of Montmartre*. c. 1886. Oil. Vincent van Gogh Foundation, Laren. The bright sunshine of Paris in spring and summer lifted Van Gogh's spirits. Even more responsible for his cheerful outlook were the heady influences of the Impressionists and the colors of Japanese prints. Moreover the bright roofs of Paris seemed a better subject to the young Dutchman than the bleak fields of the Brabant. In this painting the delicate linear patterns trace a scene in a manner that betrays the influence of the Impressionist broken-color technique combined with the fragile calligraphic style of oriental art.

10. *The Tree (after a print by Hiroshige)*. 1886. Gemeentemuseum, Amsterdam. The dappled brushwork of the Impressionists' painting is replaced by large solid areas of flat color characteristic of Japanese prints. The forcefulness of this style affected the work of both Van Gogh and Gauguin. Compare *The Tree* with Van Gogh's *L'Arlésienne* (44). Both employ large flat areas of color and both have a "scalloped edge" effect.

11. *Flowers in Bronze Vase*. 1886. Oil. The Louvre, Paris. Here Van Gogh exhibits his penchant for mixing styles of brushwork for greater textural richness. In the background he employs the stipple technique used by the Neo-Impressionists such as Seurat and Signac. The table is painted with the long parallel strokes that mark Vincent's later style. In this painting the artist has deliberately flouted the rules of perspective, again suggesting the influence of Japanese prints.

12. *Sunflowers*. 1887. Oil. Rijksmuseum Kröller-Müller, Otterlo. Yellow to the Impressionists was one of the myriad colors of sunlight. To Vincent it was to be a symbol of the life force of nature. This work, earlier thought to be a product of his stay in Arles, is now known to have been painted in Paris or on a short jaunt into the countryside near the capital.

13. *Still-Life with Mackerel*. 1886–87. Oil. Private Collection, Winterthur. Again Vincent abandons the light effects of the Impressionists. The artist is not concerned with representing the effects of light on objects, but the objects themselves.

14. *Montmartre*. 1886. Oil. Rijksmuseum Kröller-Müller, Otterlo. This was painted soon after his arrival in Paris. The landscape is still enveloped in the sullen hues of his Nuenen period.

15. *The Restaurant*. 1887. Oil. Rijksmuseum Kröller-Müller, Otterlo. Restaurants and cafés played an important role in the life of Van Gogh, as they did in the lives of his contemporaries. The painting is executed

in accordance with the laws of contrasting complementary colors of the pointillist technique. One can observe how Vincent has carefully opposed red and green dots in order to create a greater richness and more dazzling effect of color.

16. *Le Père Tanguy*. 1887. Oil. Private Collection, California. This portrait is of the proprietor of an art supply shop in Paris which Vincent frequented with other younger painters. In this composition, Van Gogh's bristling brushwork models the figure, yet at the same time the artist tries to retain a flat two-dimensional pattern. The flat forms of the Japanese prints in the background are outlined in red in order to accentuate their flatness; Père Tanguy is also outlined in red and for the same reason.

17. *Self-Portrait*. 1887. Oil. Rijksmuseum, Amsterdam. The portrait is executed in the broken-color technique of the Impressionists, yet Van Gogh employs it for its expressive force, not as a means of creating effects of light. Here the artist, like Rembrandt, paints a searching study of himself, a study enhanced by bristling broken strokes that underline the inner tensions of the sitter.

18. *Self-Portrait*. 1886–87. Oil. Gemeentemuseum, The Hague. Executed on the back of a still-life painted in Holland, this work was once thought to be a product of Van Gogh's Nuenen period. It is now known to have been executed in Paris.

19. *Nude*. 1887. Oil. Private Collection, Wassanaar. One of the few studies of the nude figure that he executed. This painting demonstrates the uncompromising realism of the Dutchman's style. It is characteristic of Van Gogh to extract the most expressive qualities from the things he represents, be they figures or landscapes.

20. *Head of a Woman*. 1887. Oil. Kunstmuseum, Basel. In this portrait Van Gogh has created a harmony of complementaries such as were advocated by the Neo-Impressionists. While rich orange-reds

dominate the portrait, green is introduced as a complementary color in order to make the orange-red appear more dazzling. He has not only introduced green in the garment but employs it in the hair and in the "whites" of the eyes.

21. *Tambourine Girl.* 1887. Oil. Vincent van Gogh Foundation, Laren. Artists found suitable subjects for their paintings in the cafés of Paris. Here Van Gogh has painted a "casual" portrait typical of the works of the Impressionists. However Van Gogh had begun painting portraits of this type at Nuenen. He is merely continuing to paint people in the attitudes in which he finds them.

22. *Woman in a Field of Grass.* 1887. Private Collection, New York. The yellow brilliance of the sun spills over into this landscape of color. In this sketch the artist has captured the fleeting moment of light and brilliant color that interested the Impressionists.

23. *Wheatfield with Lark.* 1887. Vincent van Gogh Foundation, Laren. This landscape painted near Paris seems to indicate that the artist was not altogether satisfied with painting the city and its life. The rich, shredded yellows of the wheatfield captured his attention. The vitality of the landscape presages that found in his later views at Arles, Saint-Rémy and Auvers.

24. *Souvenir de Mauve.* 1888. Oil. Rijksmuseum Kröller-Müller, Otterlo. Of this work painted in Arles Van Gogh wrote, "This may be the best landscape I ever painted." He executed it in memory of his cousin Mauve, the artist, who died in March, 1888.

25. *Le Pont de l'Anglois, Arles.* 1888. Oil. Rijksmuseum Kröller-Müller, Otterlo. The painting has the simplicity of design of Japanese prints. At the time this was painted, Van Gogh was feeling quite pleased about his work. He wrote Theo that he felt his current paintings were much improved over those he had executed a year before.

26. *Drawbridge.* 1888. Oil. Wallraf-Richartz Museum, Cologne. A bridge similar to that in (25). Perhaps the abstract design of the landscape is felt more forcefully here than in the previous painting.

27. *Young Lady of Arles.* 1888. Oil. Rijksmuseum Kröller-Müller, Otterlo. Once more the influence of Japanese prints can be observed. Vincent places the figure to the left of the canvas so that the composition is over-balanced to one side. This asymmetrical organization of the composition is typical of the Japanese print. Moreover he uses the large, flat areas of abstract color bounded by dark lines, which also characterize this style. He has broken the flat areas of color with little spots of complementaries. For example, he stipples green paint over the pink background and blue over the yellow of the garment.

28. *The Village of Saintes-Maries.* 1888. Oil. Rijksmuseum Kröller-Müller, Otterlo. In the summer of 1888 he traveled to this little village not far from Arles. While the Impressionists would have painted this scene fragmented by light, Vincent has chosen to build up the forms as a series of colored cubes, not unlike the landscape forms in Cézanne's painting.

29. *Fishing Boats at Saintes-Maries.* 1888. Oil. Vincent van Gogh Foundation, Laren. Van Gogh wrote to his friend Emile Bernard that he had at last seen the Mediterranean at Saintes-Maries. "On the flat, sandy beach little green, red, blue boats, so beautiful in shape and color that they made you think of flowers." However, the treatment of the subject recalls a Japanese print.

30. *Haystacks of Provence.* 1888. Oil. Rijksmuseum Kröller-Müller, Otterlo. For Van Gogh anything was a suitable subject for painting. Here the artist's golden haystacks seem to pulsate with inner life.

31. *La Mousmé.* 1888. Oil. National Gallery, Washington. *Mousmé* was Vincent's French version of the Japanese *musume*, meaning daughter. The artist has combined a bold composition with a simple but rich harmony of complementary colors.

32. *The Postman Roulin*. 1888. Oil. Museum of Fine Arts, Boston. The artist seems to have captured the pose of the postman at a particular instant in time. The effect is much like that achieved by photography. Van Gogh said of Roulin that he was "so natural, so intelligent in excitement and argues with such sweep in the style of Garibaldi."

33. *The Zouave*. 1888. Oil. Private Collection, New York. The model was a French officer in the Algerian corps. The simplicity and richness of the color is very striking. However the viewer is conscious that the artist has distorted the perspective of the floor which seems to slip away from beneath the feet of the soldier. This "tipped" perspective was borrowed from Japanese prints and was employed by the artist to emphasize the flatness and two-dimensional design of the painting.

34. *Painter on a Tarascon Street*. 1888. Oil. Stedelijk Museum, Amsterdam. In August Van Gogh portrays himself on his way to paint at the outskirts of town. By painting the shadow an intense blue-black to contrast with the yellow, he has created the impression of dazzling sunlight.

35. *Oleanders*. 1888. Oil. Private Collection, New York. Throughout his life, Vincent, as a spiritural heir of the northern Renaissance, sought the truth of nature in her complexity of parts.

36. *Sunflowers*. 1888. Oil. Tate Gallery, London. Van Gogh felt the sunflower was a good still-life subject. Its yellow brilliance and unusual form fascinated him. In a letter to Theo he confided, "The sunflower is mine in a way."

37. *The Night Café*. 1888. Oil. Private Collection, New York. Van Gogh thought the café a place "where one can ruin one's self, go mad or commit a crime." He felt that in this painting he was trying "to express the terrible passions of humanity by means of red and green." The harsh light of the gas lamps, which appear like miniature suns, creates an atmosphere of stark unreality.

38. *Outdoor Café at Night.* 1888. Oil. Rijksmuseum Kröller-Müller, Otterlo. "I am very interested in the idea of painting night scenes on the spot and actually by night," Vincent wrote. This work, as described by the artist, is "the terrace of a café at night, lit up by a big gas lantern, with a patch of blue, star-filled sky."

39. *The Sower.* 1888. Oil. Vincent van Gogh Foundation, Laren. This richly-colored landscape is a strange combination of reminiscences of Millet's *Sower* and Japanese prints.

40. *The Bridge of Trinquetaille.* 1888. Oil. Private Collection, New York. Vincent described this view as being executed on a grey morning: "The stones, the asphalt, the pavements are grey, the sky pale blue, the figures colored, and there is a sickly tree with yellow foliage."

41. *Van Gogh's Bedroom at Arles.* 1888. Oil. Art Institute, Chicago. Kept in by rain, Van Gogh could not ignore his brush for even one day; he painted everything in sight.

42. *Field of Grapes.* 1888. Oil. Rijksmuseum Kröller-Müller, Otterlo. Of this work Vincent exclaimed: "Oh! My study of vineyards, I have worked like a slave over it, but I have got it, again a canvas of 30 square, and again for the decoration of the house. The vines I have painted are green, purple and yellow, with violet bunches and branches of black and orange."

43. *Armand Roulin.* 1888. Oil. Folkwang Museum, Essen. This young man, son of the postman, was another member of the family that sat for Vincent. In this portrait the artist has completely given up the broken strokes and color of the Impressionists, preferring to work in the large flat areas of color found in the Japanese print.

44. *L'Arlésienne.* 1888. Oil. Metropolitan Museum of Art, New York. This portrait clearly shows the influence of the Japanese block print. Large unrelieved areas of color are contrasted one with the other.

The scalloped edges are similar to those found in Vincent's interpretation of Hiroshige's *Tree* (10).

45. *Street in Arles*. 1888. Oil. Private Collection, New York. Yellow is often the predominating tone in Vincent's Arles landscapes. Here the scene is swathed-in brilliant yellows and oranges which seem to emit their own light.

46. *Mme. Roulin and Child*. 1888. Oil. Private Collection, New York. Once more yellow is the dominating hue. The composition is again under the influence of oriental art, as Madame Roulin is cut off by the frame in the manner of figures in Japanese prints.

47. *Sunset near Arles*. 1888. Oil. Kunstmuseum, Winterthur. This dramatic landscape depicts a couple standing alone in yellow wheat at sunset. The loneliness and isolation of the figures may reflect the state of the artist's own life at this time.

48. *A Promenade at Arles*. 1888. Oil. The Hermitage, Leningrad. This landscape emulates the style of Gauguin with its large simplified areas, unbalanced composition and high eye level. However the vibrant pointillist technique was definitely Vincent's idea.

49. *Van Gogh's Chair*. 1888. Oil. National Gallery, London. Van Gogh felt that a humble chair was worthy of painting, especially when it was his own. As in (33), Vincent has tipped the floor in order to emphasize the two-dimensional pattern of the work.

50. *Gypsy Camp*. 1888. Oil. Musée de l'Impressionisme, Paris. By keeping the foreground and sky flat and devoid of forms, Van Gogh was able to concentrate the interest around the caravans, figures and horses. This compositional manipulation he learned from Japanese prints.

51. *Fruit in Basket with Gloves*. 1889. Oil. Private Collection, Amsterdam. This is generally considered to be one of the first works he

painted after returning from the hospital where he had been confined following his attempt to murder Gauguin. We may believe that Van Gogh essayed this still-life in an effort to calm his mind and prove his ability to think clearly.

52. *Still-life with Drawing Board*. 1889. Oil. Rijksmuseum Kröller-Müller, Otterlo. In January, Van Gogh executed several still-life paintings while remaining hidden from inquisitive townspeople in his little yellow house.

53. *Self-Portrait with Bandaged Ear*. 1889. Oil. Private Collection, Chicago. While regaining his sanity the artist painted this penetrating self-portrait. The rich dark green of his coat is contrasted with the vivid red and orange-red of the background. The brilliance of the reds, the bristling strokes of his fur cap and his piercing eyes all underline the intensity of the artist's expression.

54. *The Schoolboy, Camille Roulin*. 1889. Fine Arts Museum, Sao Paulo. As in the previous work, the artist has experimented with an intense red background which forces the body of the figure into strong relief. The awkward, unstable pose is emphasized by the pulsating colors of the background.

55. *La Berceuse*. 1889. Oil. Rijksmuseum Kröller-Müller, Otterlo. Unlike the two previous portraits, this work experiments with a richly patterned background against which the artist foils the large, simple masses of his model. Vincent described this painting to Theo: "A woman in green with orange hair stands out against a background of green with pink flowers."

56. *Iris*. 1889. Oil. Private Collection, New York. Probably painted near the hospital at Saint-Rémy. Vincent still sought to paint intimate portraits of nature. As he struggled to bring out the character of his sitters, so he also attempted to uncover the inner vitality of nature.

57. *The Crau at Arles: Peach Trees in Blossom.* 1889. Oil. Courtauld Institute, London. Using again broad expanses of sky and field in the foreground, Vincent makes the air come alive with brightness by freely adapting the pointillist technique to his own uses.

58. *Garden of the Hospital at Arles.* 1889. Oil. Private Collection, Winterthur. Although burdened by the knowledge of his mental condition, Vincent was able to paint an optimistic study of the hospital garden.

59. *Starry Night.* 1889. Oil. Museum of Modern Art, New York. A glimpse of how nature appeared to his fevered imagination. Here the landscape and sky seem to throb with mystical excitement. It is in a canvas such as this that landscape forms begin to take on a new expressive force.

60. *Blue Wheatfields.* 1889. Oil. National Gallery, Prague. This landscape is a much more sober view of reality. However, even here in daylight, one can detect a certain rhythmic convulsion that disturbs the tranquility of a summer day.

61. *Cypresses.* 1889. Oil. Rijksmuseum Kröller-Müller, Otterlo. The wavy, distorted lines which he loved so much are used to portray his favorite tree, with its branches reaching up to a somewhat ominous sky. Van Gogh exclaimed, "Landscapes with cypresses! Ah, it would not be easy. Aurier feels it too, when he says that even black is a color, and as for their appearance of flame—I think about it, but don't dare to go further...." The cypresses have become emotional equivalents of his own experience.

62. *The Postman Roulin.* 1889. Oil. Rijksmuseum Kröller-Müller, Otterlo. A more formal portrait of Roulin than (32). The beard that was formerly stiff and bristling, now writhes like Vincent's cypresses.

63. *Pietà (after Delacroix).* 1889. Oil. Vincent van Gogh Founda-tion, Laren. Among Van Gogh's favorite artists throughout his life

were Delacroix, Daumier, Rembrandt and Millet. Van Gogh referred to Delacroix as the father of modern painting.

64. *Self-Portrait.* 1889. Oil. Private Collection, New York. This late portrait has not the strength of color found in (53) but has a much greater formal vitality. This is due to the rhythmic flame-like shapes which the artist picks out in his smock, beard, hair and background.

65. *View with Olive Trees.* 1889. Oil. Private Collection, New York. The landscape is distorted by the rhythmic undulation of the topography. Landscape forms, rather than colors, are now the expressive force in his paintings. Vincent wrote that the trees, clouds and mountains were "exaggerations from the point of view of arrangement, their lines are distorted as in ancient woods."

66. *Wheatfield with Cypress.* 1889. Oil. Tate Gallery, London . The cypress was as dear to Vincent as the sunflower. He felt that he alone could see the true form of the tree. The cypress' flame-like shape counteracts the horizontal undulations of landscape and clouds.

67. *Pine Trees.* 1889. Oil. Rijksmuseum Kröller-Müller, Otterlo. The strong flat pattern of branches against the sky is reminiscent of Japanese prints, yet the broken brushwork is like that of the Impressionists.

68. *A Corner of the Hospital, Saint-Rémy.* 1889. Oil. Rijksmuseum Kröller-Müller. While confined here, the artist was treated kindly, having two rooms to himself and being permitted to make frequent excursions outside the asylum precincts. This work executed in the garden of the hospital betrays the broken colors of the Impressionists, except that Van Gogh used less brilliant colors and has introduced black.

69. *Peasant Binding Sheaves (after Millet).* 1889. Oil. Stedelijk Museum, Amsterdam. In his last period Vincent again sought inspiration from Millet. The peasants that were subjects of his early canvases

appear again, but now in an environment of bright color.

70. *Ploughed Field.* 1889. Oil. Private Collection, New Jersey. Perhaps tiring of asylum life, and undoubtedly appalled by the thought of a winter inside hospital walls, Van Gogh painted this post-harvest scene of empty, broken fields with a setting sun.

71. *Poppy Field.* 1889. Oil. Rijksmuseum Kröller-Müller, Otterlo. This view of a poppy field seems to look back to the work of the Impressionists. The strong touches of red vibrate over a green and yellow ground. Typical of the landscapes of this period is the high eye level which minimizes the importance of the sky.

72. *The Enclosed Field..* 1890. Oil. Rijksmuseum Kröller-Müller, Otterlo. In this landscape, as in (70) and (71), the artist has employed a high eye level. However here the artist has consciously emphasized the pattern that the land creates, making use of the design principle of the Japanese print.

73. *Portrait of an Actor.* 1889–90. Oil. Rijksmuseum Kröller-Müller, Otterlo. This portrait, full of character, recalls the style of *L'Arlésienne* (44). The same strong surface pattern is employed as well as the scalloped edges.

74. *The Good Samaritan (after Delacroix).* 1890. Oil. Rijksmuseum Kröller-Müller, Otterlo. Because of frequent attacks and his consequent need of isolation, Vincent painted innumerable copies of works of art he admired. The rhythmic vitality of Delacroix's figures must have been particularly attractive to him when his own works were alive with similar undulating forms.

75. *Chestnut Tree in Blossom.* 1890. Oil. Rijksmuseum Kröller-Müller, Otterlo. Vincent was always fond of flowers, whether as subject of a still-life or part of a landscape. The flowering tree provided a rich pattern of color with luxuriant greens broken by the white fragments

28

of blossoms.

76. *The Church at Auvers*. 1890. Oil. Musée de l'Impressionisme, Paris. A heavy blue sky provides an ominous background to this strange, contorted church, which seems to writhe on an unsteady foundation. Van Gogh combines strong, almost abstract color with distorted forms to provide a dramatic, expressive statement of his inner conflicts.

77. *Boats*. 1890. Oil. Rijksmuseum Kröller-Müller, Otterlo. The subject matter, the color and treatment seem to harken back to the sparkling canvases of the Impressionists.

78. *Stairway at Auvers*. 1890. Oil. Municipal Art Museum, St. Louis. In this period the convulsion of landscape forms becomes more noticeable. Van Gogh consciously emphasizes the movement of the landscape by outlining forms in dark color.

79. *L'Arlésienne*. 1890. Oil. Rijksmuseum Kröller-Müller, Otterlo. This painting was based on a drawing by Gauguin. Vincent has employed gentle curves in contrast to the hard angular lines that occur in (44).

80. *Dr. Gachet's Daughter Playing the Piano*. 1890. Oil. Kunstmuseum, Basel. Hoping, perhaps, to portray the peaceful life of the family which represented his only link with normal life in Auvers, Vincent painted this richly harmonious portrait. He used some of the technique of pointillism combined with the strong rhythmic outlines and compositional devices of the Japanese print. This work seems to foreshadow paintings of Edvard Munch.

81. *Undergrowth*. 1890. Oil. Private Collection. This is one of many canvases of his later period in which two people appear. Vincent described this work as a "view under poplars, violet trunks, which cross the landscape perpendicularly like columns, the depths of the wood are blue and under the great trunks the flowers white, rose, yellow and

green...."

82. *Girl of Auvers*. 1890. Oil. Museum of Fine Arts, San Francisco. A study of a girl painted very broadly in simple complementary colors, yellow and blue.

83. *Child Holding Orange*. 1890. Oil. Private Collection, Winterthur. As soft and as gentle as these colors are, we can see in Van Gogh's background and in the treatment of the figure that the artist is still able to produce a portrait that is both bold and dramatic. The background meadow seems to flow up around the figure, forming a rich flowered setting for the portrait.

84. *Cypress and Starry Sky with Road*. 1890. Oil. Rijksmuseum Kröller-Müller, Otterlo. Harkening back to his days in the Midi (and perhaps painted there), Van Gogh recreates his road of life winding tortuously into space and marked by his favorite tree, the cypress. Of this work Vincent wrote, "I have....a cypress with a star, a last attempt—a night sky with a moon without radiance, the slender crescent barely emerging from the opaque shadow cast by the earth—a star with exaggerated brilliance, if you like, a soft brilliance of rose and green in the ultramarine sky across which clouds are hurrying."

85. *The Farmer's Daughter*. 1890. Oil. Private Collection, Winterthur. Van Gogh's contrast of flat areas of bright color is similar to that employed so often by Gauguin. The viewer seems to be looking straight ahead at the sitter, yet down upon the wheatfield. The "double viewpoint" enables the artist to use the background as a purely decorative device.

86. *Fresh Grass in a Park.*. 1890. Oil. Rijksmuseum Kröller-Müller. "My work goes well, I have done two canvases of the fresh grass in the park, one of which is extremely simple. The trunk of a pure violet pink and then the grass with white flowers and dandelions, a little rose tree and other tree trunks in the background right at the

top of the canvas."

87. *Branch of a Blossoming Chestnut Tree.* 1890. Oil. Private Collection, Zurich. A late example of Van Gogh's interest in flowers. This study like (86) reveals a desire for a close study of nature and her implicit richness of pattern.

88. *Wheatfield with Crows.* 1890. Oil. Vincent van Gogh Foundation, Laren. Despairing for his life, Van Gogh ventured into this field near Auvers to paint a picture of a road seeming to end abruptly in the middle of the field. Crows rise suddenly from the waves of grain, as if in panic. This is one of his most emotionally-charged landscapes.

89. *Thatched Cottages.* 1890. Oil. Kunsthaus, Zurich. As in his early days at Nuenen, the peasant dwelling commands his attention. Here, heavy paint gives the canvas an almost sculptured effect.

90. *Cottages at Cordeville.* 1890. Oil. Musée de l'Impressionisme, Paris. This landscape seems to writhe and twist with inner life. An example of his late work in which the expressiveness of the landscape is achieved by means of form rather than color.

91. *Portrait of Dr. Gachet..* 1890. Oil. Private Collection, New York. Between the two men, patient and doctor, artist and friend, ran an undercurrent of trust and compassion. In this late work the rhythmic curves are enforced by the parallel brush strokes which seem to stream over and around the figure of the doctor.

VINCENT VAN GOGH

1853   Born on March 30, at Groot-Zundert, a Dutch village near the Belgian border, to Theodorus van Gogh, a Protestant minister.

1857   Birth of Theo, Vincent's favorite brother, on May 1.

1869   On July 30, begins work at Goupil art gallery in The Hague.

1872   First record of exchange of letters with Theo.

1873–74   In May, transferred to the Goupil branch in London. Falls in love with his landlady's daughter but is rejected by her. In July returns home for holidays in a depressed mood.

1875–76   Transferred to Paris office in May. Finds it increasingly difficult to concentrate on his work at Goupil's. Experiences a deepening interest in the Bible. In April, he is released from Goupil's. Travels to England to teach school at Ramsgate and then at Isleworth on the outskirts of London, eventually serving as a kind of curate. Sees a future working with people, perhaps as missionary or preacher.

1877   For the first four months of the year, he is a bookshop employee in Dordrecht, but is studying, hoping to prepare for a career in the Church. Moves to Amsterdam to prepare for theological examinations.

1878–79   Gives up studies but enters lay evangelical school in Brussels. Volunteers for missionary service in the Borinage. In July, he is relieved of a probationary posting at Wasmes. Remains in Borinage at his own expense.

1880   Wanders over the countryside of Belgium and the Netherlands, occasionally drawing peasants and copying works by Millet.

October, he is in Brussels. Studies anatomy and devotes himself to drawing.

1881   In April, returns to Etten to live with parents. Falls in love with young widowed cousin Kee, who refuses his advances. December, leaves for The Hague. Receives encouragement from Anton Mauve, a painter.

1882   January, meets prostitute Christien ("Sien"), who will be model and mistress for nearly two years. In June receives commission for pen-and-ink sketches of The Hague. Occupied with studies of peasants. Begins painting in oil.

1884   Love affair with Nuenen girl who attempts suicide. Among the paintings executed at this time are *The Weaver* (1), *The Loom* (2), and *Still-Life with Hat and Pipe* (4).

1885   In March, Vincent's father dies suddenly. This year he paints *The Potato Eaters* (6), *Peasant Woman* (5) and *The Open Bible* (7). In late November, leaves for Antwerp.

1886   Enters Academy at Antwerp, but soon leaves for Paris where he lives with Theo. Paints, among other canvases, *Montmartre* (8), *The Tree* (10), and *Flowers in a Bronze* Vase (11). Meets Toulouse-Lautrec and Emile Bernard.

1887   Meets Pissarro, Degas, Seurat, Gauguin and Signac. Among his Paris canvases are *Sunflowers* (12), *The Restaurant* (15), *Le Pere Tanguy* (16), *Self-Portrait* (17), *Nude* (19), *Head of a Woman* (20), *Woman in Field of Grass* (22) and *Wheatfield with Lark* (23).

1888   In Arles in February. Wishes to establish an artists' colony. Moves in May to his "little yellow house." In June, spends a week at Saintes-Maries on the Mediterranean where he paints *Fishing Boats at Saintes-Maries* (29). In October, Gauguin arrives. In December, he tries to kill Gauguin, then cuts off part of his own right ear. Van Gogh's production during this period includes *Le Pont de L'Anglois* (25), *Drawbridge* (26),

Young Lady of Arles (27), *Village of Saintes-Maries* (28), *Haystacks of Provence* (30), *La Mousmé* (31), *The Zouave* (33), *The Postman Roulin* (32), *Oleanders* (35), *Sunflowers* (36), *The Night Café* (37), *The Sower* (39), *The Bridge of Trinquetaille* (40), *Van Gogh's Bedroom at Arles* (41), *Mme. Roulin and Child* (46), *Sunset Near Arles* (47), *Van Gogh's Chair* (49) and *Gypsy Caravan* (50).

1889 Released from hospital on January 7, Van Gogh returns to his little house and paints *Self-Portrait with Bandaged Ear* (53), *La Berceuse* (55), *Fruit in Basket with Gloves* (51) and *Still-Life with Drawing Board* (52). In February, neighbors have him recommitted. On May 9, at his own request, Vincent enters the asylum at Saint-Rémy. Other canvases he executed this year include, *Iris* (56), *The Crau at Arles* (57), *Garden of the Hospital at Arles* (58), *Starry Night* (59), *Blue Wheatfields* (60), *Cypresses* (61), *Postman Roulin* (62), *Wheatfield with Cypress* (66), *Pine Trees* (67), *Peasant Binding Sheaves* and *Poppy Field* (71).

1890 In January, the art critic Aurier publishes the first criticism of his work in the *Mercure de France,* praising him enthusiastically. The first and only painting by him to be sold during his lifetime is purchased for 400 francs at a Brussels exhibition organized by the group, "Les Vingt." On May 21, Van Gogh arrives at Auvers-sur-Oise, a village just north of Paris. July 27, shoots himself near the wheatfields he had painted just a few days before. Two days later he dies. Theo, in ill health collapses and dies six months later. The two brothers are buried side by side in the cemetery at Auvers. Among the canvases executed at Auvers were *The Church at Auvers* (76), *Boats* (77), *Stairway at Auvers* (78), *Dr. Gachet's Daughter Playing the Piano* (80), *Undergrowth* (81), *Girl of Auvers* (82), *Child Holding Orange* (83), *Wheatfield with Crows* (88) and *Portrait of Dr. Gachet* (90).

LIST OF COLOR PLATES

1. The Weaver. 1884.
2. The Loom. 1884.
3. Snowy Day. 1884.
4. Still-Life with Hat & Pipe. 1884.
5. Peasant Woman. 1885.
6. The Potato Eaters. 1885.
7. The Open Bible. 1885.
8. Montmartre. 1886.
9. A Corner of Montmartre. c. 1886.
10. The Tree (after Hiroshige). 1886.
11. Flowers in a Bronze Vase. 1886.
12. Sunflowers. 1887.
13. Still-Life with Mackerel. 1886-87.
14. Montmartre. 1886.
15. The Restaurant. 1887.
16. Le Père Tanguy. 1887.
17. Self-Portrait. 1887.
18. Self-Portrait. 1886-87.
19. Nude. 1887.
20. Head of a Woman. 1887.
21. Tambourine Girl. 1887.
22. Woman in Field of Grass. 1887.
23. Wheatfield with Lark. 1887.
24. Souvenir de Mauve. 1888.
25. Le Pont de l'Anglois, Arles. 1888.
26. Drawbridge. 1888.
27. Young Lady of Arles. 1888.
28. Village of Saintes-Maries. 1888.
29. Boats at Saintes-Maries. 1888.
30. Haystacks of Provence. 1888.
31. La Mousmé. 1888.
32. The Postman Roulin. 1888.

33. The Zouave. 1888.
34. Painter on a Tarascon Street. 1888.
35. Oleanders. 1888.
36. Sunflowers. 1888.
37. Night Cafe. 1888.
38. Outdoor Cafe at Night. 1888.
39. The Sower. 1888.
40. The Bridge of Trinquetaille. 1888.
41. Van Gogh's Bedroom at Arles. 1888.
42. Field of Grapes. 1888.
43. Armand Roulin. 1888.
44. L'Arlesienne. 1888.
45. Street in Arles. 1888.
46. Mme. Roulin and Child. 1888.
47. Sunset near Arles. 1888.
48. Promenade at Arles. 1888.
49. Van Gogh's Chair. 1888.
50. Gypsy Camp. 1888.
51. Fruit in Basket with Gloves. 1889.
52. Still-Life, Drawing Board. 1889.
53. Self-Portrait with Bandaged Ear. 1889.
54. The Schoolboy Roulin. 1889.
55. La Berceuse. 1889.
56. Iris. 1889.
57. The Crau at Arles. 1889.
58. Garden of Hospital, Arles. 1889.
59. Starry Night. 1889.
60. Blue Wheatfields. 1889.
61. Cypresses. 1889.
62. The Postman Roulin. 1889.
63. Pietà (after Delacroix). 1889.

35

64. Self-Portrait. 1889.
65. View with Olive Trees. 1889.
66. Wheatfield with Cypress. 1889.
67. Pine Trees. 1889.
68. A Corner of the Hospital, Saint-Rémy. 1889.
69. Peasant Binding Sheaves (after Millet). 1889.
70. Ploughed Field. 1889.
71. Poppy Field. 1889.
72. Enclosed Field. 1890.
73. Portrait of an Actor. 1889-90.
74. The Good Samaritan (after Delacroix). 1890.
75. Chestnut Tree in Blossom. 1890.
76. The Church at Auvers. 1890.
77. Boats. 1890.

78. Stairway at Auvers. 1890.
79. L'Arlésienne. 1890.
80. Dr. Gachet's Daughter Playing the Piano. 1890.
81. Undergrowth. 1890.
82. Girl of Auvers. 1890.
83. Child Holding Orange. 1890.
84. Cypress and Starry Sky with Road. 1890.
85. The Farmer's Daughter. 1890.
86. Fresh Grass in a Park. 1890.
87. Branch of Blossoming Chestnut. 1890.
88. Wheatfield with Crows. 1890.
89. Thatched Cottages. 1890.
90. Cottages at Cordeville. 1890.
91. Portrait of Dr. Gachet. 1890.

THE PLATES

1 *The Weaver*. 1884. Oil. 18⅞ × 18⅛ in. Private Collection, Berlin. A man of great compassion, Van Gogh was always concerned for the peasant and his lot.

2 *The Loom*. 1884. Oil. 27½ × 33⅜ in. Rijksmuseum Kröller-Müller, Otterlo. Vincent found that the weaver and his loom made an excellent subject for painting.

3 *Snowy Day*. 1884. Oil. 26½ × 49½ in. Private Collection, Laren. The dark earth colors helped to suggest the closeness of the peasant to the soil which sustained him.

4 *Still-Life with Hat and Pipe.* 1884. Oil. 14½ × 21 in. Rijksmuseum Kröller-Müller, Otterlo. The artist painted still-life subjects throughout his career.

5 *Peasant Woman*. 1885. Oil. 16⅛ × 12⅜ in. Private Collection, Zurich. Van Gogh, like Rembrandt, attempted to capture the very soul of his sitter.

6 *The Potato Eaters*. 1885. Oil. $32\frac{1}{4} \times 44\frac{7}{8}$ in. Vincent van Gogh Foundation, Laren. The early Van Gogh often chose the somber colors of Rembrandt and Millet.

7 *The Open Bible.* 1885. 25½ × 30¾ in. Vincent van Gogh Foundation, Laren. After the artist's failure as a missionary he came to Nuenen to live.

8 *Montmartre*. 1886. Oil. 17⅜ × 13¼ in. Art Institute, Chicago. In February, 1886, he moved to Paris and began to paint in brighter colors.

9 *A Corner of Montmartre.* c. 1886. Oil. 13¾ × 25¼ in. Vincent van Gogh Foundation, Laren. Japanese prints and Impressionism helped to open a new world of design and color to him.

10 *The Tree (after a print by Hiroshige).* 1886. Oil. 22 × 18⅛ in. Gemeentemuseum, Amsterdam. An attempt to capture the Japanese aesthetic concepts.

11 *Flowers in a Bronze Vase.* 1886. Oil. 28⅞ × 23⅝ in. The Louvre, Paris. This work betrays the influences of Impressionist and Neo-Impressionist techniques.

12 *Sunflowers*. 1887. Oil. 19½×38¼ in. Rijksmuseum Kröller-Müller, Otterlo. One of the first of many sunflower compositions he was to paint.

13 *Still-Life with Mackerel.* 1886-87. Oil. 14¾×21½ in. Private Collection, Winterthur. Van Gogh tried desperately to sell his paintings, without success.

14 *Montmartre*. 1886. Oil. 14⅜ × 17⅞ in. Rijksmuseum Kröller-Müller, Otterlo. Never an
orthodox Impressionist, he is often hailed as a precursor of Expressionism.

15 *The Restaurant*. 1887. Oil. 17¾ × 21¼ in. Rijksmuseum Kröller-Müller, Otterlo. The influence of Seurat and Signac is seen in his technique of pointillism.

16 *Le Père Tanguy*. 1887. 24⅞ × 20⅛ in. Private Collection, California. M. Tanguy was both friend and champion of the younger artists who rejected the teachings of the Academy.

17 *Self-Portrait*. 1887. Oil. 16⅛ × 12⅝ in. Rijksmuseum, Amsterdam. The bristling brush-strokes which are evident here will become even more apparent in his later work.

18   *Self-Portrait.*   1886-87. Oil. 20½ × 16¾ in. Gemeentemuseum, The Hague. The sharp penetrating eyes reveal something of the artist's tormented sensibility.

19 *Nude*. 1887. Oil. 9½ × 16⅛ in. Private Collection, Wassanaar. The influence of Impressionism appears here but the colors foreshadow the artist's more mature palette.

20 *Head of a Woman*. 1887. Oil. 16½×13 in. Kunstmuseum, Basel. Van Gogh always employed large areas of pure color for their strong emotional impact.

21 *Tambourine Girl*. 1887. Oil. 21¾×18¼ in. Vincent van Gogh Foundation, Laren. The decorative element of post-Impressionism seems to have had an influence on Van Gogh.

22 *Woman in Field of Grass*. 1887. Oil. 16⅜×13⅝ in. Private Collection, New York. Here he has captured all the brilliance of light found in the canvases of the Impressionists.

23 *Wheatfield with Lark*. 1887. Oil. $21\frac{3}{8} \times 25\frac{3}{8}$ in. Vincent van Gogh Foundation, Laren. The artist tries to convey his love of nature.

24 *Souvenir de Mauve*. 1888. Oil. 28⅝ × 23⅜ in. Rijksmuseum Kröller-Müller, Otterlo. In
Arles, Van Gogh continues to experiment with color and light.

25 *Le Pont de l'Anglois, Arles.* 1888. Oil. 20⅝ × 24¾ in. Rijksmuseum Kröller-Müller, Otterlo. The influence of the Japanese print is still very evident.

26 *Drawbridge*. 1888. Oil. 20½ × 26½ in. Wallraf-Richartz Museum, Cologne. Another bridge study.

27 *Young Lady of Arles*. 1888. Oil. 19⅝ × 19⅜ in. Rijksmuseum Kröller-Müller, Otterlo. He lodged at a cafe where he painted many of the customers.

28 *The Village of Saintes-Maries*. 1888. Oil. $25\frac{1}{8} \times 20\frac{5}{8}$ in. Rijksmuseum Kröller-Müller.
In early summer he painted this view from the fields behind Saintes-Maries.

29 *Fishing Boats at Saintes-Maries*. 1888. Oil. 25⅜ × 31⅞ in. Vincent van Gogh Foundation, Laren. The brightness of the sky and blue of the sea impressed him deeply.

30 *Haystacks of Provence*. 1888. Oil. 29×36¼ in. Rijksmuseum Kröller-Müller. His infatuation with the blinding sun and brilliant colors began to transform his art.

31 *La Mousmé*. 1888. Oil. 28¾ × 23¾ in. National Gallery, Washington. He portrays a village
girl in the richness of color found in Japanese prints.

32　*The Postman Roulin.*　1888.　Oil.　31¼ × 25 in.　Museum of Fine Arts, Boston.　Van Gogh met Roulin in August and soon had painted the entire family.

33 *The Zouave.* 1888. Oil. $31\frac{7}{8} \times 25\frac{1}{2}$ in. Private Collection, New York. Van Gogh said: "The portrait is the form which brings out the best in me."

34 *Painter on a Tarascon Street*. 1888. Oil. 19 × 17⅜ in. Stedelijk Museum, Amsterdam. In Arles Van Gogh exhausted himself painting incessantly.

35 *Oleanders*. 1888. Oil. 23½ × 28⅝ in. Private Collection, New York   He continued to experiment with color in his still-life paintings.

36 *Sunflowers*. 1888. Oil. 37⅜ × 28⅝ in. Tate Gallery, London. Sunflowers, like the sun,
became an important element of his paintings of the Arles period.

37 *The Night Café.* 1888. Oil. 27½ × 35 in. Private Collection, New York. The artist has captured a haunting sense of isolation that was to permeate his later landscapes.

38 *Outdoor Café at Night.* 1888. Oil. 31 × 24¾ in. Rijksmuseum Kröller-Müller. Painted in
September after a month spent drawing bright fields of wheat.

39 *The Sower*. 1888. Oil. $13\frac{1}{4} \times 16\frac{1}{8}$ in. Vincent van Gogh Foundation, Laren. Compared to his early works of peasants in Nuenen, this is quite optimistic in feeling.

40 *The Bridge of Trinquetaille*   1888.   28½×36½ in.   Private Collection, New York.   This scene is one of two of the same view.

41 *Van Gogh's Bedroom at Arles*. 1888. Oil. 28⅜ × 35⅞ in. Art Institute, Chicago. When inclement weather confined him, he would paint his room or the objects it contained.

42 *Field of Grapes*. 1888. Oil. 27⅞ × 35½ in. Rijksmuseum Kröller-Müller, Otterlo. Painted shortly before Gauguin came to live with him in the autumn.

43 *Armand Roulin*. 1888. Oil. 25½ × 21¼ in. Folkwang Museum, Essen. The subject is shown here in a subdued shade of the artist's favorite color, yellow.

44 *L'Àrlésienne*. 1888. Oil. 35⅜ × 28¼ in. Metropolitan Museum of Art, New York. This portrait of Mme. Ginoux is very oriental in feeling.

45 *Street in Arles*. 1888. Oil. 35 × 28⅜ in. Private Collection, New York. Poplar trees drenched in the brilliant yellow of autumn.

46 *Mme. Roulin and Child*. 1888. Oil. 25 × 20⅛ in. Private Collection, New York. Van Gogh enjoyed being with the Roulins as they were very kind to him.

47 *Sunset near Arles*. 1888. Oil. 29⅛ × 35⅞ in. Kunstmuseum, Winterthur. A canvas of rich subdued colors suggesting a mood of loneliness.

48 *A Promenade at Arles.* 1888. Oil. 28⅝ × 36¼ in. The Hermitage, Leningrad. An unusual
composition painted under the influence of Gauguin.

49 *Van Gogh's Chair*. 1888. Oil. 35⅜ × 27⅞ in. National Gallery, London. The colors of wall, door and floor provide strong background contrast.

50 *Gypsy Camp*. 1888. Oil. 16⅛ × 20. Musée de l'Impressionisme, Paris. This scene is characteristic of the colorful canvases of the Arles period.

51 *Fruit in Basket with Gloves.* 1889. Oil. 18⅝ × 24⅛ in. Private Collection, Amsterdam. With still-life subjects he could work more slowly and deliberately when not feeling well.

52 *Still-Life with Drawing Board.* 1889. Oil. 19⅝ × 25⅛ in. Rijksmuseum Kröller-Müller.
Painted in January, when he despaired of his sanity.

53 *Self-Portrait with Bandaged Ear*. 1889. Oil. $20 \times 17\frac{5}{8}$ in. Private Collection, Chicago.
Painting helped to release the tensions that built up inside of him.

54 *The Schoolboy, Camille Roulin.* 1889. Oil. 24¾ × 21¼ in. Museum of Fine Arts, Sao Paulo. The same intense red background occurs here as in (53.)

55 *La Berceuse*. 1889. Oil. 36¼ × 28 in. Rijksmuseum Kröller-Müller, Otterlo. Painted before he suffered more hallucinations and was again confined to a hospital.

56 *Iris*. 1889. Oil. 28¾ × 37 in. Private Collection, New York. The artist always enjoyed painting flowers.

57 *The Crau at Arles: Peach Trees in Blossom.* 1889. Oil. 25⅞ × 32 in. Courtauld Institute, London. Painted in April, before requesting asylum at Saint-Rémy.

58   *Garden of the Hospital at Arles.*   1889.   Oil.   28¾ × 36⅛ in.   Private Collection, Winterthur.   This is the hospital to which he was first confined.

59 *Starry Night*. 1889. Oil. 28⅝ × 36⅛ in. Museum of Modern Art, New York. The swirling meteors emit an unearthly glow above his favorite cypress trees.

60 *Blue Wheatfields*. 1889. Oil. 28¾ × 36⅜ in. National Gallery, Prague. Again his favorite
subjects: wheatfields and cypress trees.

61 *Cypresses*. 1889. Oil. $35\frac{7}{8} \times 27\frac{7}{8}$ in. Rijksmuseum Kröller-Müller, Otterlo. The writhing forms of the cypresses can be found in many canvases of the Arles period.

62 *The Postman Roulin*. 1889. Oil. 25½ × 21¼ in. Rijksmuseum Kröller-Müller, Otterlo. The postman sat many times for Van Gogh.

63 *Pietà (after Delacroix)*. 1889. Oil. 28¾ × 23¾ in. Vincent van Gogh Foundation, Laren.
The artist often copied works of his favorite painters when confined by weather or illness.

64 *Self-Portrait*. 1889. Oil. 22½ × 17¼ in. Private Collection, New York. Van Gogh worked
continually in spite of long periods of depression.

65 *View with Olive Trees*. 1889. Oil. $28\frac{3}{8} \times 36\frac{1}{4}$ in. Private Collection, New York. On his painting excursions, he favored cypresses, mountains and olive orchards.

66 *Wheatfield with Cypress.* 1889. Oil. 28⅝ × 36 in. Tate Gallery, London. His later landscapes seem to throb with an inner life.

67 *Pine Trees*. 1889. Oil. 35⅜ × 27⅞ in. Rijksmuseum Kröller-Müller, Otterlo. This landscape reflects the influence of the Japanese print.

68 *A Corner of the Hospital, Saint-Rémy.* 1889. Oil. 37⅜ × 29¾ in. Rijksmuseum Kröller-Müller.
The doctors of the Arles and Saint-Rémy hospitals encouraged him to paint.

69 *Peasant Binding Sheaves (after Millet)*. 1889. Oil. 17 × 13½ in. Stedelijk Museum, Amsterdam. Borrowing from Millet, he painted this and other compositions of his beloved wheatfields.

70 *Ploughed Field.* 1889. Oil. 27⅞ × 35⅜ in. Private Collection, New Jersey. The increasingly depressed artist enjoyed painting the open fields.

71 *Poppy Field*. 1889. Oil. 28¾ × 36⅝ in. Rijksmuseum Kröller-Müller, Otterlo. This landscape recalls the work of the Impressionists.

72 *Enclosed Field*. 1890. Oil. 27⅞ × 35⅞ in. Rijksmuseum Kröller-Müller, Otterlo. The interesting pattern of fields indicates further influence of the Japanese print.

73 *Portrait of an Actor*. 1889-90. Oil. 25½ × 21¼ in. Rijksmuseum Kröller-Müller, Otterlo. A very penetrating study which in style resembles (44).

74 *The Good Samaritan (after Delacroix).* 1890. Oil. 28⅜×23⅛ in. Rijksmuseum Kröller-Müller, Otterlo. He became concerned with religious themes while in the asylum.

75 *Chestnut Tree in Blossom.* 1890. Oil. 24 × 18⅞ in. Rijksmuseum Kröller-Müller, Otterlo. An example of Van Gogh's consuming interest in the intricate patterns of nature.

76 *The Church at Auvers.* 1890. Oil. 36⅜ × 29½ in. Musée de l'Impressionisme, Paris. A landscape reflecting the inner conflicts of the artist.

77 *Boats*. 1890. Oil. 23 × 36¼ in. Rijksmuseum Kröller-Müller, Otterlo. A work in the tradition
of the Impressionists.

78 *Stairway at Auvers*. 1890. Oil. 18⅞×27⅝ in. Municipal Art Museum, St. Louis. The landscape is composed almost entirely of curved lines.

79 *L'Arlésienne*. 1890. Oil. 24¾ × 18½ in. Rijksmuseum Kröller-Müller, Otterlo. Painted after
a composition by Gauguin.

80 *Dr. Gachet's Daughter Playing the Piano.* 1890. Oil. 40¼×19½ in. Kunstmuseum, Basel. The artist was very close to the Gachets and especially devoted to the doctor.

81 *Undergrowth*. 1890. Oil. 19⅝ × 39¼ in. Private Collection. The couple can be found in other paintings as early as those of the Arles period.

82 *Girl of Auvers*. 1890. Oil. 25⅞ × 21⅜ in. Museum of Fine Arts, San Francisco. A bold study in yellows and blues.

83 *Child Holding Orange*. 1890. $20\frac{3}{8} \times 18\frac{1}{4}$ in. Private Collection, Winterthur. Very pale in color this work contrasts with the rich hues of canvases of the Arles period.

84 *Cypress and Starry Sky with Road*. 1890. Oil. 35⅞×27⅞ in. Rijksmuseum Kröller-Müller, Otterlo. Van Gogh has created a strange new vision of the night.

85　*The Farmer's Daughter*.　1890.　Oil.　$36\frac{1}{4} \times 28\frac{5}{8}$ in.　Private Collection, Winterthur.　Often Van Gogh loved to include his beloved fields in the backgrounds of portraits.

86 *Fresh Grass in a Park*. 1890. Oil. 28⅜ × 35⅜ in. Rijksmuseum Kröller-Müller, Otterlo. One of his intimate studies of a confined piece of ground.

87 *Branch of a Blossoming Chestnut Tree.* 1890. Oil. $28\frac{3}{8} \times 36\frac{5}{8}$ in. Private Collection, Zurich.
The strong pattern reminds one of the designs of Japanese prints.

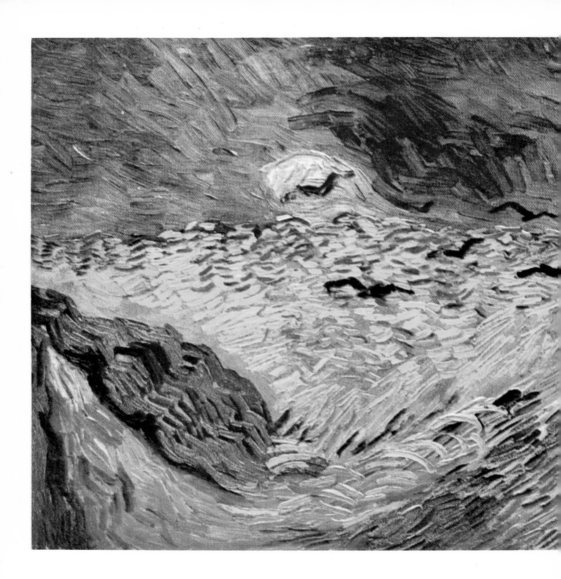

88 *Wheatfield with Crows*. 1890. Oil. 20×40¾ in. Vincent van Gogh Foundation, Laren. The artist's last work, painted not far from the spot where he shot himself.

89 *Thatched Cottages*. 1890. Oil. Kunsthaus, Zurich. Although painted in Auvers, this scene is typical of the hovels of Holland and Belgium which he never forgot.

90 *Cottages at Cordeville*. 1890. Oil. 28⅜ × 35⅞ in. Musée de l'Impressionisme, Paris. Another study of a similar subject.

91 *Portrait of Dr. Gachet.* 1890. Oil. 25⅞ × 22⅜ in. Private Collection, New York. An amateur painter himself, Dr. Gachet proved a good friend.